ORDINARY DAYS

For Skipper.

For Amiir.

For the Northside.

ORDINARY DAYS

THE SEEDS, SOUND, AND CITY
THAT GREW PRINCE ROGERS NELSON

written by Angela Joy

illustrated by Jacqueline Alcántara

Roaring Brook Press
New York

In spring,
sometimes before the last April snow,
wild lilacs begin to grow.
They press their way through cracks and crevices,
seeking sun.

Their blush will turn leftover streets into a symphony of lavender hue,
    whispering on the wind that beauty is found in every thing
        and every one . . .
            even the ordinary day.

On ordinary days, you could see him:
a beautiful boy, but small,
with a smile given only to lilacs
growing between broken sidewalks,
carrying in his pockets
a sound.

Hard and round, he carried sound like seeds or lucky pennies,
broken rhymes and memories that with rain would one day grow:

Mama's hum,
dishes clanking,
shouts and silence,
slamming doors.

Papa's song,
rhythms playing,
trilling now through feet and floors—
wanting more.

More than the sound he could hear but never, ever touch.

The boy wrapped fear and wanting into pockets
to wait for a rainy day.

On ordinary days, you could see him:
a catch of breath in mittens, threadbare,
feasting on what he could smell in the air but couldn't afford to buy.
Dreaming the dreams of ordinary things a boy would like to try:
milkshakes,
french fries.
But all he had was sun,
purring pigeons,
passing cars.

The boy wrapped sunshine and hunger into pockets
to wait for a rainy day . . .

But the waiting wasn't easy without roots.
Without an ordinary home to call his own,
the boy blew 'round like a petal on the wind:

Mama's house,
Auntie's house,
Papa's place, too small.
Sometimes lonely,
sometimes angry,
sometimes lost in basketball.

The beautiful boy belonged everywhere
and nowhere
at all.

Papa bought him a new guitar.
It was the best that he could do.
Music was the boy's most faithful friend.

With radio and records,
with lessons from mentors at a place called "The Way,"
the beautiful boy listened,
he learned how to play every song, every riff, every sound.

Soon he met other kids who could hear the music, too.
Together they made a band: Grand Central.
The band practiced in André's basement.

André was a great friend.

His mom, Ms. Bernadette, was a great friend, too.
She let the boy stay there.
On warm, welcoming pillows, her house became his home.

With Ms. Bernadette's laughter just upstairs,
the boy wrapped roots and "thank you" into pockets
to wait for a rainy day.

And when the clouds finally came, they felt like home.

Eyes closed, guitar in hand,
surrounded by rhythm, by blues, by the band,
the boy began to play what he'd been hiding deep in pockets.
Tender shoots of seed and sound broke ground.

Shouts and silence,
slamming doors;
whispering lilacs,
basement floors;
the thud of a basketball,
boom-boom;
the echo of lonely in a
crowded room.

JAMES BROWN

JIMI HENDRIX

SLY AND THE FAMILY STONE

A secret wink, the warmth of blush,
Papa's stride and Mama's touch,
the purr of pigeons, hunger pain,
the color of sky as it contemplates rain . . .

. . . sadness, friendship, faith, and fear,
he released into the atmosphere
where just outside the crowd could hear
the rain come
down, down.

With lightning's flash the boy could see
the man that he would grow to be.
With rain, and sun, and harmony, he'd be a star.
The world would sing his sound out loud—
the beautiful boy called Prince would be proud

of the name his parents gave him.
Standing on stages, near and far,
he'd drive the band and
drive the fast car;
he'd learn that love would make him tall, but—

not today.

Today was meant for being small.
For sowing seeds of song into storm.
The clouds wrapped 'round to keep him warm
while the extraordinary

became just another ordinary
day.

On ordinary days, you could see him:
a beautiful boy, but small,
in a world so loud and fast and tall,
carrying in his pockets a song . . .

AUTHOR'S NOTE

PRINCE ROGERS NELSON was born in Minneapolis, Minnesota, on June 7, 1958. Poor, Black, small in stature, and prone to seizures, Prince was an unlikely candidate for a cultural icon. He was named for his father's jazz band, the Prince Rogers Trio, but the nickname "Skipper" seemed a better fit.

Skipper and his younger sister, Tyka, enjoyed an early exposure to music; Mom's voice and Dad's piano were regular sources of enrichment in their home. Yet the children were strictly prohibited from touching the household piano. For Skipper, this restriction only increased his desire to play.

Punctuated by arguments and occasional violence, the Nelson union was tumultuous. The couple split up when Prince was seven. He spent the ensuing years living with various relatives and friends. It was during this time that Prince developed a deep devotion to basketball, playing competitively on the Bryant Junior High and Central High School teams. Yet music was his constant. When not practicing piano, drums, or synthesizer in rehearsal spaces, Prince could be found at the Northside community center, The Way. There he honed bass and electric guitar skills, absorbing all he could from master musicians like Craig Peterson and Sonny Thompson. By the time he was fourteen, Prince was proficient enough to perform with adult musicians, a welcome distraction from ongoing personal matters. Unable to get along with his parents, Prince was allowed to move in with his best friend, André. André's mother, neighborhood matriarch Bernadette Anderson, gave Prince a structured safe haven, where good behavior was expected and creativity was celebrated. Under Ms. Bernadette's watch, Prince graduated high school, and his tremendous talent bloomed. While attending Minneapolis Central High, Prince helped create a cover band named Grand Central. With André "Cymone" Anderson, Linda Anderson,

William "Hollywood" Doughty, Morris Day, and Terry Jackson, the group performed at parties, nightclubs, and in the legendary "Battle of the Bands." The fierce competition among talented young musicians sharpened skill and spurred creativity, birthing a genre that would later be known as the Minneapolis Sound. Perfected by Prince, this synthesized mesh of funk, jazz, soul, folk, and rock was musically distinct and revolutionary, putting Prince in a class of his own as he departed for LA.

Prince landed his first recording contract at the age of eighteen. Hedging their bets, Warner Music executives planned to enlist Maurice White, famed founder of the band Earth, Wind & Fire, to produce the inaugural project. Additional instrumentalists were also on tap to professionally record the music. Yet with uncanny ability and a healthy slice of arrogance, Prince convinced the execs that he could write, perform, and produce the album entirely on his own. The project, *For You*, begins with an a cappella harmony stack—a vocal commitment to share life, memory, and music with his listeners. From these very first notes until his last, Prince Rogers Nelson delivers.

The early years weren't easy for Prince. *For You* showed only moderate success. At a particularly low point, audience members threw trash and racist, homophobic slurs at the band while they opened for the Rolling Stones. Prince was reportedly crushed, but he didn't give up. With incomparable determination, the beautiful boy, but small, churned out album after album, persona after persona, band after band, to become a living legend. Still, countless accomplishments could not silence the residual effects of a difficult childhood. Destructive relationships with God, self-esteem, and fame were pervasive, often wounding those in his ever-changing inner circle. Long-term relationships remained elusive as two failed marriages, familial estrangements, and the tragic death of a son lingered quietly in the background.

Yet through it all, the music was there. In time, Prince found footing in his faith. A devoted Jehovah's Witness, he attended service at a local church and conducted door-to-door ministry with his neighbors; his lyrics and interviews reflected a newfound sense of peace.

On April 21, 2016, overcome by pain medication, Prince Rogers Nelson died within his Minnesota estate, Paisley Park. In the days that followed, bridges, stadiums, and monuments around the world shone purple as mourners of all ages and ethnicities gathered to grieve. Yet nowhere was the shock more acute than in Minneapolis—particularly North Minneapolis, where he had spent his "ordinary days." There, Prince was more than a local celebrity. He was ours. Unexpected sightings, pop-up parties, "anonymous" donations, and childhood friendships made us feel as if we were a part of his life, part of his journey, stockholders in his success. He felt like a friend.

Shortly after Prince's death, I was contacted by a classmate from fourth grade. She sent a note of condolence, remembering how much I loved Prince; how I used to sing "Baby I'm a Star" on the soccer field at Jefferson Elementary! Even after decades without contact, she knew his death would be devastating for me, because it was devastating for us all. In publishing what started as a tribute poem for his son, I hope to celebrate what Prince gave to me: the audacity to dream BIG no matter where you come from, and a deep devotion to the *art* and expression of music. In my eyes, Prince was a wildflower that broke through racism, poverty, and abuse to turn our leftover streets into a symphony of lavender hue, reminding me that beauty can be found even in the ashes of our ordinary days.

PRINCE: A FAMILY PLAYLIST

"For You"—*For You*, 1978

"Free"—*1999*, 1982

"Purple Rain"—*Purple Rain*, 1984

"Let's Go Crazy"—*Purple Rain*, 1984

"I Would Die 4 U"—*Purple Rain*, 1984

"Baby I'm a Star"—*Purple Rain*, 1984

"God"—"Purple Rain" single B side, 1984

"17 Days"—"When Doves Cry" single B side, 1984

"Paisley Park"—*Around the World in a Day*, 1985

"Sometimes It Snows in April"—*Parade*, 1986

"Starfish and Coffee"—*Sign o' the Times*, 1987

"Play in the Sunshine"—*Sign o' the Times*, 1987

"Sign o' the Times"—*Sign o' the Times*, 1987

"Batdance"—*Batman* (movie soundtrack), 1989

"The Morning Papers"—*Love Symbol*, 1992

"Sweet Baby"—*Love Symbol*, 1992

"4 the Tears in Your Eyes"—*The Hits/The B-Sides*, 1993

"The Most Beautiful Girl in the World"—*The Gold Experience*, 1995

"Don't Talk 2 Strangers"—*Girl 6* (movie soundtrack), 1996

Published by Roaring Brook Press
Roaring Brook Press is a division of Holtzbrinck Publishing Holdings Limited Partnership
120 Broadway, New York, NY 10271 ◆ mackids.com

Library of Congress Control Number 2022920829
ISBN 978-1-250-79703-2

Our books may be purchased in bulk for promotional, educational, or business use.
Please contact your local bookseller or the Macmillan Corporate and Premium
Sales Department at (800) 221-7945 ext. 5442 or by email at
MacmillanSpecialMarkets@macmillan.com.

First edition, 2023
The illustrations for this book were done primarily in watercolor with some details rendered in
marker and adjustments made in Adobe Photoshop. The main typeface is Adobe Jenson Pro.
The book was edited by Connie Hsu, designed by Mike Burroughs, and art directed by
Sharismar Rodriguez. The production was managed by Celeste Cass and Elizabeth Peskin, and
the production editors were Jennifer Healey and Hayley O'Brion. Printed in China by
RR Donnelley Asia Printing Solutions Ltd., Dongguan City, Guangdong Province.

1 3 5 7 9 10 8 6 4 2